I BELIEVE

Help thou mine unbelief

Laurence Muzembi

SIMPLE GOSPEL SUMMATIONS

*Biblical advice for new and
growing Christians*

PREFACE

I believe is for you who say Lord I believe, but you continue to face life uncertainties, and pressure, shame, anxiety, trouble, failure, worriment and botheration. You say Lord; I believe but help thou my unbelief. You are probably saying like that same man at the pool of Bethesda, there was "...I have no man, when the water is troubled, to put me into the pool: but while I am coming, another steppeth down before me..." John 5:5-9. This book will probably lead to your betterment. We read in Proverbs 13:12, "Hope deferred maketh the heart sick: but when the desire cometh, it is a tree of life."

Do yourself a huge favour today, pick up your courage and run to the Lord. "The name of the Lord is a strong tower: the righteous runneth into it, and is safe." Proverbs 18:10. Here is how you run to him, say Lord I believe.

Run to him with what's bothering you; that inconvenience, ado, aggravation, annoyance, anxiety, bellyache, care, concern, difficulty, distress, drag, exasperation, flurry, fuss, headache, irritant, irritation, molestation, nudge, nuisance, pain, perplexity, pest, plague, strain, trial or vexation

Paul says, "Nay, in all these things we are more than conquerors through him that loved us. For I am persuaded, that neither death, nor life, nor angels, nor principalities, nor powers, nor things present, nor things to come, Nor height, nor depth, nor any other creature, shall be able to separate us from the love of God, which is in Christ Jesus our Lord." Romans 8:35-39

It doesn't matter that your hope was delayed, deferred, interrupted, adjourned, detained, or discontinued because he says come; "he that sat upon the throne said, Behold, I make all things new. And he said unto me, Write: for these words are true and faithful." Revelation 21:5

Jehoshaphat stood up and said, "Hear me, O Judah, and ye inhabitants of Jerusalem; Believe in the Lord your God, so shall ye be established; believe his prophets, so shall ye prosper." 2 Chronicles 20:20

It's your day today, say I believe, and he will give you rest.

"Hear me, O Judah, and ye inhabitants of Jerusalem; Believe in the Lord your God, so shall ye be established; believe his prophets, so shall ye prosper." 2 Chronicles 20:20

I BELIEVE - PART I

H ear me, O Judah, and ye inhabitants of Jerusalem; Believe in the Lord your God, so shall ye be established; believe his prophets, so shall ye prosper" (2 Chr. 20:20).

I repeat these words, *"Believe in the Lord your God, so shall ye be established; believe his prophets, so shall ye prosper."* I believe in God, I believe also his prophets those who are indeed prophets of his much in every way. Proverbs 26:25 also says, *"When he speaketh fair, believe him not: for there are seven abominations in his heart"*. Watch out for these abominations.

One thing God blessed us believers with, is the ability to see and hear aright. That's right, he teaches you good judgment and knowledge so you can believe what's that good and acceptable to Him. Not every reporter has good news for you. *"The simple believeth every word: but the prudent man looketh well to his going."* Proverbs 14:15

God called us that we may only BELIEVE IN him, and not to believe everything or every word said concerning him by whoever, but only those he's sent. He said to Job's three friends, *"My wrath is kindled against thee, and against thy two friends: for ye have not spoken of me the thing that is right, as my servant Job hath"* Job 42:7.

The problem with some believers is they're quick to believe every word said by their favourite preachers yet slow to believe the written word. They trust their teachers more than they trust God. Jesus said, *"O fools, and slow of heart to believe all that the prophets have spoken: Ought not Christ to have suffered these things, and to enter into his glory?"* Luke 24:25-26.

The prophets spoken here are of course not the ones there these days who *"savourest not the things that be of God, but the things that be of men."* These prophets of old were different, for with one voice they spoke *"...that believe on his name"* John 1:12.

Believest thou on him?

Jesus himself said; *"Let not your heart be troubled: ye believe in God, believe also in me."* John 14:1. He didn't say believe in Peter, James and John or any of my disciples, but he said believe in me.

I believe that I AM is he, and him only we should serve.

Of all I've written about today here is the sum, BELIEVE IN God; *"He that believeth on him is not condemned: but he that believeth not is condemned already, because he hath not believed in the name of the only begotten Son of God"* John 3:18.

I said believe in God, but the question is what's there to believe in?

In the book of Genesis we've Abram, one such representing all of us who've undertaking this journey of believing. Something extraordinary happened to him, *"...the word of the Lord came unto Abram in a vision..."* Genesis 15:1.

It's the same word such as you hear these days, but when it first came to Abram it came in a form of a vision. It doesn't have to be for you but the effects are the same; it is alive, powerful and active, though it's in written form. The same spirit works in you both to will and to do.

Looking at our scripture, the word came to Abram while he was surrounded with fear, worry and troubles of his own, and probably it's the same with you. When the word came, (not God, not an angel nor a man of God) "*...he believed in the Lord; and he counted it to him for righteousness.*" Genesis 15:6.

You see why John 1:1-3 says, "*In the beginning was the Word, and the Word was with God, and the Word was God. The same was in the beginning with God. All things were made by him; and without him was not anything made that was made.*"

What's pastor saying?

I hear Jesus say, "*Have I been so long time with you, and yet hast thou not known me, Philip? he that hath seen me hath seen the Father; and how sayest thou then , Shew us the Father? Believest thou not that I am in the Father, and the Father in me? the words that I speak unto you I speak not of myself: but the Father that dwelleth in me, he doeth the works. Believe me that I am in the Father, and the Father in me: or else believe me for the very works' sake.*" John 14:9-11

Anyway to cut the long story short, the Word is God, it's it to believe, my friend. Abram, believing the same word which came to him he believed in the Lord through the same.

What was the word?

"*...Fear not, Abram: I am thy shield, and thy exceeding great reward.*" Genesis 15:1.

It was no vain word!

To give you a little background to the story, the bible says in the previous chapter war filled the whole land. Kings fought against each other in Abram's days, and worse also Abram had provoked them by rescuing Lot. Obviously at some point there was going to be payback time. That's the reason why the Word of the Lord came to him, it was to reassure him.

War was all around. You hear that friend; war is all around, and on top of that, own life battles. Abram said, *"O, Lord God, what wilt thou give me, seeing I go childless?"* Genesis 15:2.

I hear David say, *"I had fainted, unless I had believed to see the goodness of the Lord in the land of the living."* Psalm 27:13. Believing is incompatible with fear.

When we say fear not, we're not saying be positive. All we are saying is, see the word, see the goodness of the Lord. Know and believe the love that God has for you. He's *"thy shield, and thy exceeding great REWARD."* Preachers aren't motivational speakers at all; but behold, we bring you life eternal, we bring you good tidings of great joy - practically speaking, it's the Word of God that comes to you. *"Unto you therefore which believe he is precious..."* 1 Peter 2:7.

When Abram heard of rewards, he replied, *"O Lord Jehovah, what good are all your blessings when I have no son? For without a son, some other member of my household will inherit all my wealth"* Genesis 15:2-3.

You don't want sister, brother cousin or in-law to inherit your wealth; you want your own child. It's no fun feelings we want when we pray.
No, not excitement but you look into the future. It's cash flow we want, and to achieve, and legacy to leave for our children and generations to come, and life hereafter. That's the reason why we go to church. The purpose is not to seek excitement, but is seeing visions.

Then the Lord told him, *"No, no one else will be your heir, for you will have a son to inherit everything you own."*

Hear me friend; YOU WILL HAVE that you believe God for. Don't be fearful, He will defend you, and will give you great blessings.

It's said in verse 6, *"And Abram believed God; then God considered him righteous on account of his faith."*

"...without faith it is impossible to please him: for he that cometh to God must believe that he is, and that he is a rewarder of them that diligently seek him." Hebrews 11:6.

Abram believed; I believe, what would you? Fear not, friend!

I BELIEVE - PART II

The word of the Lord came to Abram carrying a specific message for him, "...*This shall not be thine heir; but he that shall come forth out of thine own bowels shall be thine heir. And he brought him forth abroad, and said, Look now toward heaven, and tell the stars, if thou be able to number them: and he said unto him, So shall thy seed be.*" Genesis 15:4-5.

He didn't have to twist scriptures like some of us do to suit his conditions. Some believers are only good at stealing other people's birthrights. They've no personal relationship with God themselves except to claim this and that scripture and deceive, and calling that faith/believing. The word of God has to come to you my friend.

"...*this shall not be thine heir; but he that shall come forth out of thine own bowels...*"

It has to come from the abundance of your own heart; from your own cistern, devotions, and connection with the spirit of Christ.

I hear Solomon say, "*Trust in the Lord with all thine heart; and lean not unto thine own understanding*" Proverbs 3:5.

To help you understand, Jesus said, "*As for these things which ye behold, the days will come, in the which there shall not be left one stone upon another, that shall not be thrown down"* Luke 21:6.

Why? It shall be tested by fire; even your own faith, and it better be genuine faith, otherwise that you see, trust, or lean on *"shall not be left one stone upon another."*

Your present circumstances shall certainly not be your heir, but that you shall become as a result of trusting in God is what matters. It takes me back to creation; the present earth was *"without form, and void; and darkness were upon the face of the deep."* But when He spoke, things that needed to be happened - there was light. And yourself, the things that shall be are not done yet, only believe and they'll make haste to happen also.

Here is how; the spirit will move upon everything you've believed God for.

And he brought him forth abroad, and said, look now toward heaven, and tell the stars, if thou be able to number them: and he said unto him, so shall thy seed be.

Don't look upon your present circumstances. The Lord said, *"Take heed, and beware of covetousness: for a man's life consisteth not in the abundance of the things which he possesseth"* Luke 12:15. Look towards heaven! He said, *"Look now toward heaven, and tell the stars, if thou be able to number them."*

If you look toward heaven and you're able tell, most likely you've not seen aright. It's highly probable that most of our own life achievements have not been as a result of God's connection, and therefore are not reckoned of grace, but of debt.

"For we are saved by hope: but hope that is seen is not hope: for what a man seeth, why doth he yet hope for?" Romans 8:24. Even faith, is not faith when you see it, or if it's within your reach. If thou not be able to number them: *"he said unto him, so shall thy seed be."*

I like this; *"Wherefore also it is contained in the scripture, Behold, I lay in Sion a chief corner stone, elect, precious: and he that believeth on him shall not be confounded."* 1 Peter 2:6

"And he believed in the Lord; and he counted it to him for righteousness." Genesis 15:6.

Paul asks, *"How then shall they call on him in whom they have not believed? And how shall they believe in him of whom they have not heard? And how shall they hear without a preacher? And how shall they preach, except they are sent?"* Romans 10:14-15

Preachers preach: you hear what's to be heard, believe on him they preach about, and then call upon him they've preached about.

Abram believed in the Lord. We saw even how the word came to him, and yourself friend, you need to also believe that same word coming to you about him. Just not good enough to know there is God; believe that he is, and that He rewards all those who diligently seek him. There has to be a dialogue between you with him, and believing or trusting him is a good way forward.

How then shall they call on him in whom they have not believed?

People ask, how can I pray effective prayers? First, read the word, believe also in the same word. After you've done that, you're now able to pray according to his will. It's His word, and believing that makes you able to pray effective prayers. Effective prayers are prayed according to his will. Don't we pray Thy will be done...?

And he [Abram] believed in the Lord; and he [God] counted it to him for righteousness.

"...he counted it to him for righteousness."

"But to do good and to communicate forget not: for with such sacrifices God is well pleased." Hebrews 13:16.

A believer should always communicate with his God; God is also pleased with such sacrifices and commitment. For *"How then shall they call on him in whom they have not believed? And how shall they believe in him of whom they have not heard?"*

I BELIEVE - PART III

*A*nd he believed in the Lord; and he counted it to him for right-*eousness. And he said unto him, I am the Lord that brought thee out of Ur of the Chaldees, to give thee this land to inherit it. And he said, Lord God, whereby shall I know that I shall inherit it? And he said unto him, Take me an heifer of three years old, and a she goat of three years old, and a ram of three years old, and a turtledove, and a young pigeon."* Genesis 15:6-9

When Abram believed in the Lord it also transformed his thinking. He learned to rely on God. He said, Lord God, whereby shall I know that I shall inherit it? Henceforward, Abram knew where to look for spiritual help. He knew he needed no human mentor for he had just gotten rid of Lot.

People globetrot when faced with difficult questions like these. I pity preachers who when called by God don't feel sufficient of their own calling. Some think to affiliate with old prophets is the answer, so they cross borders begging for spiritual help.
Let me help you preacher; Abram *"believed in the Lord; and he counted it to him for righteousness."*

When he wasn't sure how, he went back to God and said, *"Lord God, whereby shall I know that I shall inherit it?"* The reason we go back to him is he's the author and finisher of his work.

When he went back, the Lord said, take me an heifer! Tell me, who of your counsellors and advisors and mentors would be able to advice you like this? I guess they'll say be like me; *"proclaim a fast and say God told me this year is the year of constructing tarred roads."* But believe them not if they shall prophesy to you what man also are capable of doing.

Learn to give honour or respect to whom it is due. If your president gives you tarred roads; it's him not God. I hear Jesus say, *"Render therefore unto Caesar the things which are Caesar's; and unto God the things that are God's"* Matthew 22:21. Here is what a true prophecy looks like; a virgin shall bear a son, or *"Look now toward heaven, and tell the stars, if thou be able to number them: and he said unto him, So shall thy seed be"* Genesis 15:5. Now, that's what God's own prophecies are like - he exceedeth all our expectations, it's beyond any shadow of doubt my friend.

The Lord said to Abram, take me an heifer! It means what he is about to do cannot be replicated or reversed; no magician can do it. It's going to be, just.

The bible says Abram took those sacrifices and then the Lord said to him, *"Know of a surety..."* Genesis 15:10, 13. And the same day the Lord made a covenant with Abram, Genesis 15:18. Hallelujah!

I hear Paul say, *"And be renewed in the spirit of your mind; and that ye put on the new man, which after God is created in righteousness and true holiness."* Ephesians 4:23-24, if so be ye have tasted that the Lord is gracious.

Abram *"believed in the Lord; and he counted it to him for righteousness."* Not of our own, but God's righteousness. There is a difference between what man can do and what God can, fasting and starving, knowing there is God and believing. As believers, we must demonstrate those differences.

I BELIEVE - PART IV

*A*nd when Abram was ninety years old and nine, the Lord appeared to Abram, and said unto him, I am the Almighty God;
walk before me, and be thou perfect. And I will make my covenant between me and thee, and will multiply thee exceedingly." Genesis 17:1-2

God appeared to Abram and told him, walk before me, obey me
and live as you should, i.e., be perfect.

As long as you live right you will also be blessed, God will multiply you exceedingly. He said I will make my covenant between
me and you stand, and I will continue this agreement between us
generation after generation, forever, for it shall be between me
and your children as well. *"It is a contract that I shall be your God and
the God of your posterity."*

The Psalmist said;

*Who shall ascend into the hill of the Lord? Or who shall stand in his
holy place? He that hath clean hands, and a pure heart; who hath not
lifted up his soul unto vanity, nor sworn deceitfully. He shall receive
the blessing from the Lord, and righteousness from the God of his salvation. This is the generation of them that seek him that seek thy face,
O Jacob. Selah. Lift up your heads, O ye gates; and be ye lift up, ye everlasting doors; and the King of glory shall come in. Who is this King of*

glory? The Lord strong and mighty, the Lord mighty in battle." Psalm 24:3-8

You want to receive a blessing from the Lord? First, believe! Accept that he said is true. You don't have to have proof. Secondly, seek his face, have clean hands, and a pure heart. Do not lift up your soul to all desires of your will, self obsession, self absorption, self centeredness, egotism, pride nor swear deceitfully.

"What's more," God told Abram, *"I am changing your name. It is no longer 'Abram' ('Exalted Father'), but 'Abraham' ('Father of Nations') - for that is what you will be. I have declared it."* Genesis 17:5. Henceforth, it's not your petty desires that should motivate you, for this is what you will be - Father of Nations.

God said, *"As for me, behold, my covenant is with thee, and thou shalt be a father of many nations."* Genesis 17:4

"And I will give unto thee, and to thy seed after thee, the land ... for an everlasting possession; and I will be their God....Thou shalt keep my covenant therefore, thou, and thy seed after thee in their generations." Genesis 17:8-9.

There is nothing too hard for the Lord, and if you believe, all things are possible to you who believe, *"And blessed is she that believed: for there shall be a performance of those things which were told her from the Lord."* Luke 1:45

He was just Abram, but not anymore!
His name is no more 'Abram' ('Exalted Father'), but 'Abraham' ('Father of Nations') - for that is what you will be, and God said I have declared it. This also became of you since you believed. We're blessed together with faithful Abraham in Christ. Galatians 3:6-9 says, *"Even as Abraham believed God, and it was accounted to him for righteousness. Know ye therefore that they which are of faith, the same are the children of Abraham. And the scripture, foreseeing that God would justify the heathen through faith, preached*

before the gospel unto Abraham, saying, In thee shall all nations be blessed. So then they which be of faith are blessed with faithful Abraham."

Abraham had the same experience -God declared him fit for righteousness only because he believed God's promises. The real children of Abraham are all the men of faith who truly trust in God, you and me who walk before Him, obey Him and live as Abraham lived. God told Abraham about this long ago when he said, "I will bless those in every nation who trust in me as you do." And so it is: all who trust in Christ share the same blessing Abraham received.

Have a surrendered life. Abraham's life was a surrendered life, and in chapter 16 you can see how.

He listened to the voice of Sarai and went in to Hagar, and she convinced. Sarah realising her fault, *"said unto Abram, My wrong be upon thee: I have given my maid into thy bosom; and when she saw that she had conceived, I was despised in her eyes: the Lord judge between me and thee"* Genesis 16:5. What does he do? He says to her, *"Behold, thy maid is in thy hand; do to her as it pleaseth thee. And when Sarai dealt hardly with her, she fled from her face"* Genesis 16:6. A few years later when Sarah had Isaac, she sees Ishmael mocking her son, and *"she said unto Abraham, Cast out this bondwoman and her son: for the son of this bondwoman shall not be heir with my son, even with Isaac"* Genesis 21:10. What does Abraham do? He sends her away.

Sending her away was grievous but God had reassured him, saying, *"Let it not be grievous in thy sight because of the lad, and because of thy bondwoman; in all that Sarah hath said unto thee, hearken unto her voice; for in Isaac shall thy seed be called"* Genesis 21:12. He did it anyway, and took bread, and a bottle of water, and gave it unto Hagar, putting it on her shoulder, and the child, and sent her away.

It's a surrendered life that led him to want to sacrifice his son. We read, *"that God did tempt Abraham, and said unto him, Abraham: and he said, Behold, here I am"* Genesis 22:1. Believing is saying Yes,

Lord! *"Nevertheless not my will, but thine, be done"* Luke 22:42.

"And the angel of the Lord called unto him out of heaven, and said, Abraham, Abraham: and he said, Here am I. And he said, Lay not thine hand upon the lad, neither do thou any thing unto him: for now I know that thou fearest God, seeing thou hast not withheld thy son, thine only son from me. And Abraham lifted up his eyes, and looked, and behold behind him a ram caught in a thicket by his horns: and Abraham went and took the ram, and offered him up for a burnt offering in the stead of his son. And Abraham called the name of that place Jehovah-jireh: as it is said to this day, In the mount of the Lord it shall be seen. And the angel of the Lord called unto Abraham out of heaven the second time, And said, By myself have I sworn, saith the Lord, for because thou hast done this thing, and hast not withheld thy son, thine only son : That in blessing I will bless thee, and in multiplying I will multiply thy seed as the stars of the heaven, and as the sand which is upon the sea shore; and thy seed shall possess the gate of his enemies; And in thy seed shall all the nations of the earth be blessed; because thou hast obeyed my voice." Genesis 22:11-18

Believing is when God calls you and you say, Here am I. Don't be rigid, but allow yourself to be led. Remember, whatever he's leading you to, it shall be seen. *"For all the promises of God in him are yea, and in him Amen, unto the glory of God by us."* 2 Corinthians 1:20

I BELIEVE - PART V

A nd it came to pass at that time, that Abimelech and Phichol the chief captain of his host spake unto Abraham, saying, God is with thee in all that thou doest" Genesis 21:22.

When God is with you people will always see. It'll be evident that God or some supernatural power is helping you. The devil will also know! "*And the Lord said unto Satan, Hast thou considered my servant Job, that there is none like him in the earth, a perfect and an upright man, one that feareth God, and escheweth evil? Then Satan answered the Lord, and said, Doth Job fear God for nought? Hast not thou made an hedge about him, and about his house, and about all that he hath on every side? thou hast blessed the work of his hands, and his substance is increased in the land.*" Job 1:8-10

You too always you have this protection from harm around you, and your home and your property. God has blessed you so much, and from today I want you to see yourself blessed in everything that you do. Don't see a curse anymore but see God blessing the works of your hands and prospering everything that you do - see increase, "*...because he hath glorified thee*" Isaiah 60:9. In this same chapter of Isaiah it is written, "*Violence shall no more be heard in thy land, wasting nor destruction within thy borders; but thou shalt call thy walls Salvation, and thy gates Praise*" Isaiah 60:18. Instead, the forces of the Gentiles will come, but only to minister to you.

When Abimelech and Phichol the chief captain of his host spoke to Abraham, please note; they were not tricked into believing, but they came
with a testimony of how that they're defeated and they said "God is with thee in all that thou doest." Everyone should be able to see on their own that the glorious power working within us is from God and not our own doing. People should be able to see that it's Christ working in us both to will and to do of his good pleasure, and that it is him keeps us safe. Yes, we live under constant threats and danger to our lives because we believe, but this gives us constant opportunities to show forth the power of Jesus Christ within us.

We believe, "*while we look not at the things which are seen, but at the things which are not seen: for the things which are seen are temporal; but the things which are not seen are eternal.*" 2 Corinthians 4:18

And "*We having the same spirit of faith, according as it is written, I believed, and therefore have I spoken; we also believe, and therefore speak*" 2 Corinthians 4:13.

I BELIEVE - PART VI

*A*nd she called the name of the Lord that spake unto her, Thou God seest me: for she said, Have I also here looked after him that seeth me?" Genesis 16:13

Always remember this, God sees you through and through, and you'll not be disappointed if you believe in him but you'll live to tell it.

In her affliction Hagar could not even pray probably because it was her fault. Sarai had punished her, beat her up and she ran away. But God looked upon her and sent her an angel with with the good news, *"the LORD hath heard thy affliction"* Genesis 16:11.

Thereafter Hagar called on the name of the Lord, and she gave him a name, El-Roi - " *Thou God who seest me"* - for it was he who had appeared to her and looked upon her in her affliction. When you feel lonely and abandoned by people, know that God is with you. He sees you and He knows you. He hears the cry of your heart and He loves you more than you can imagine. he will lead you through and fill your heart with His praise and much hope.

Years later, she is again in trouble! Just happened day, *"Abraham rose up early in the morning, and took bread, and a bottle of water, and gave it unto Hagar, putting it on her shoulder, and the child, and sent her away: and she departed, and wandered in the wilderness of Beer-*

sheba." Genesis 21:14

Water runs out and she left the young lad in the shade to die. She couldn't pray, but all she could do was lift up her voice and cry. *"And God heard the voice of the lad; and the angel of God called to Hagar out of heaven, and said unto her, what aileth thee, Hagar? Fear not; for God hath heard the voice of the lad where he is. Arise, lift up the lad, and hold him in thine hand; for I will make him a great nation. And God opened her eyes, and she saw a well of water; and she went, and filled the bottle with water, and gave the lad drink. And God was with the lad; and he grew, and dwelt in the wilderness, and became an archer."* Genesis 21:18-20

It was not prayer God heard, but he heard the voice of the boy. What troubles you, Hagar? Do not be afraid, for God has heard the voice of the boy from where he is. When you're in trouble, he both sees, and hears your troubled voice.

The Lord said to Moses, *"...I have surely seen the affliction of my people which are in Egypt, and have heard their cry by reason of their taskmasters; for I know their sorrows; And I am come down to deliver them out of the hand of the Egyptians, and to bring them up out of that land unto a good land and a large, unto a land flowing with milk and honey; unto the place of the Canaanites, and the Hittites, and the Amorites, and the Perizzites, and the Hivites, and the Jebusites. Now therefore, behold, the cry of the children of Israel is come unto me: and I have also seen the oppression wherewith the Egyptians oppress them. Come now therefore, and I will send thee unto Pharaoh, that thou mayest bring forth my people the children of Israel out of Egypt."* Exodus 3:7-10

Paul says to Timothy, *"But thou hast fully known my doctrine, manner of life, purpose, faith, longsuffering, charity, patience, persecutions, afflictions, which came unto me at Antioch, at Iconium, at Lystra; what persecutions I endured: but out of them all the Lord delivered me."* 2 Timothy 3:10-11

What am I saying friend? It is God that'll see you through and through, and you'll not be disappointed if you believe in him but you'll live to tell it.

"For we through the Spirit wait for the hope of righteousness by faith." Galatians 5:5

Waiting on the Lord is something believers do. Being able to wait is trusting God's character and goodness. We wait expectantly and with hope, *"And hope maketh not ashamed; because the love of God is shed abroad in our hearts by the Holy Ghost which is given unto us"* Romans 5:5. To wait upon the Lord is to expect something from him in godly hope, and hope does not disappoint.

There are times when God will delay his answer, and many times we wonder when and how he's going to intervene. But, knowing God, we trust that soon he will at the perfect moment, not a second too soon or too late.

"For I reckon that the sufferings of this present time are not worthy to be compared with the glory which shall be revealed in us. For the earnest expectation of the creature waiteth for the manifestation of the sons of God. For the creature was made subject to vanity, not willingly, but by reason of him who hath subjected the same in hope, Because the creature itself also shall be delivered from the bondage of corruption into the glorious liberty of the children of God. For we know that the whole creation groaneth and travaileth in pain together until now. And not only they , but ourselves also, which have the firstfruits of the Spirit, even we ourselves groan within ourselves, waiting for the adoption, to wit, the redemption of our body. For we are saved by hope: but hope that is seen is not hope: for what a man seeth, why doth he yet hope for? But if we hope for that we see not, then do we with patience wait for it. Likewise the Spirit also helpeth our infirmities: for we know not what we should pray for as we ought: but the Spirit itself maketh intercession for us with groanings which cannot be uttered." Romans 8:18-26

The scripture above teaches us to wait with godly hope, and as we've already seen hope does not disappoint. You see how all creation eagerly awaits God's restoration: *"For the earnest expectation of the creature waiteth for the manifestation of the sons of God."* (Romans 8:19). Those who wait for God to keep His promises will not be disappointed, "Likewise the Spirit also helpeth our infirmities."

Psalm 37:34 says, *"Wait on the Lord, and keep his way, and he shall exalt thee to inherit the land: when the wicked are cut off, thou shalt see it."*

My prayer is that O Lord teach us to wait, and to wait on the Lord is to rest in the confident assurance that, regardless of the details or difficulties we face in this life, emotionally, physically or spiritually, God never leaves us without a sure defence. Paul says in 2 Corinthians 12:9, *"And he said unto me, My grace is sufficient for thee: for my strength is made perfect in weakness. Most gladly therefore will I rather glory in my infirmities, that the power of Christ may rest upon me."*

I guess you believe it is so with your own life too! Do not despair but wait on the Lord.

"Hope deferred maketh the heart sick: but when the desire cometh, it is a tree of life." Proverbs 13:12

But no matter the nature of problem; be it trouble, complication, bad situation, dilemma, dispute, headache, obstacle, questions, issues, disagreements, doubt, disputed points, worriment or difficulties - wait on God, he's bigger than any kind of trouble, concern, danger, dilemma, disappointment, distress, grief, hindrance, dire straits or any sort of bad news.

Whether it be bone of contention; altercation, discord, argument, conflict, controversy, debate, disagreement, dispute, grounds for war, issue, difference of opinion, matter at hand - believe!

In my other book I wrote a wounded spirit who can bear? I was quoting Proverbs 18:14 which says "The spirit of a man will sustain his infirmity; but a wounded spirit who can bear?"

You need to believe; and have faith, and hope in God so you can be *"strengthened with all might, according to his glorious power, unto all patience and longsuffering with joyfulness"* Colossians 1:11. The Bible says Hezekiah further strengthened his defences by repairing the wall wherever it was broken down, he strengthened his fortifications and constructed another wall outside it. You also need to do the same today; your faith needs further reinforcement, and my prayer is even when attacked your heart would be able to discover itself.

So many things, and people, and your own mind may be trying to attack your soul, *"The words of a talebearer are as wounds, and they go down into the innermost parts of the belly."* Proverbs 18:8

And yes probably you're your own enemy; *"A fool's mouth is his destruction, and his lips are the snare of his soul"* Proverbs 18:7. *"Death and life are in the power of the tongue: and they that love it shall eat the fruit thereof"* Proverbs 18:21.

But when courage dies, what hope is left?

Nothing, but shame, humiliation, embarrassment contempt, ignominy reproach, defeat, destruction, wounds, great wasting of self and to be wasted. We read Proverbs 13:12 and it says, *"Hope deferred maketh the heart sick: but when the desire cometh, it is a tree of life."*

Do yourself a huge favour today, pick up your courage and run to the Lord. *"The name of the Lord is a strong tower: the righteous runneth into it, and is safe."* Proverbs 18:10.

Run to him with that which bothers you; your trouble, inconvenience, ado, aggravation, annoyance, anxiety, bellyache, botheration, bustle, care, concern, difficulty, distress, drag, exasperation, flurry, fuss, headache, irritant, irritation, molestation, nudge, nuisance, pain, perplexity, pest, plague, pressure, problem, strain, to-do, trial, trouble, vexation, worriment, worry, whatever. That botheration; annoyance, aggravation, bothering, bugging, disturbance, exasperation, harassment, hassle, headache, inconvenience, irritation, nuisance, pestering, problem, vexation. Whether it's a bother or trouble, inconvenience, ado, aggravation, annoyance, anxiety, bellyache, botheration, bustle, care, concern, difficulty, distress, drag, exasperation, flurry, fuss, headache, irritant, irritation, molestation, nudge, nuisance, pain, perplexity, pest, plague, pressure, problem, strain, to-do, trial, trouble, vexation, worriment, worry, or a bug; glitch, breakdown, malfunction, defect, error, failure, fault, flaw, hitch, problem, something wrong, trouble.

Paul says, *"Who shall separate us from the love of Christ? shall tribulation, or distress, or persecution, or famine, or nakedness, or peril, or sword? As it is written, For thy sake we are killed all the day long; we are accounted as sheep for the slaughter. Nay, in all these things we are more than conquerors through him that loved us. For I am persuaded, that neither death, nor life, nor angels, nor principalities, nor powers, nor things present, nor things to come, Nor height, nor depth, nor any other creature, shall be able to separate us from the love of God, which is in Christ Jesus our Lord."* Romans 8:35-39

Be it a delay/delays; deferment, interruption, adjournment, dawdling, demurral, detention, discontinuation, downtime, hindrance, hold-up, holding, impediment, interval, lingering, obstruction, postponement, procrastination, prorogation, putting off, remission, reprieve, retardation, retardment, setback, suspension which has been used by the enemy as snares of death, but Proverbs 16:20 says, *"He that handleth a matter wisely shall find good: and whoso trusteth in the Lord, happy is he."*

I BELIEVE - PART VII

And Abraham said, "*My lord, if now I have found favor in your sight, please do not pass by your servant [without stopping to visit]*. Genesis 18:3

What happened here has a resemblance to what happened to the two on their way to Emmaus. "*And they talked together of all these things which had happened. And it came to pass, that, while they communed together and reasoned, Jesus himself drew near, and went with them.*" Luke 24:14-15

The only difference their eyes were holden that they should not know him but Abraham straightaway knew that they were angels.

In this journey ask God to open your eyes too so you can see. Don't wait until it's too late for you but smell it - know your day of visitation. The Bible says, "*And he [Abraham] lift up his eyes and looked, and, lo, three men stood by him: and when he saw them, he ran to meet them from the tent door, and bowed himself toward the ground, And said, My Lord, if now I have found favour in thy sight, pass not away, I pray thee, from thy servant.*" Genesis 18:2-3.

He was sitting down, God knows what was going on through his mind, but as soon as he saw these three men, he jumped, and something jumped in him too. Food is set before them, as they ate, *"they said unto him, Where is Sarah thy wife? And he said, Behold, in the tent. And he said, I will certainly return unto thee according to the time of life; and, lo, Sarah thy wife shall have a son. And Sarah heard it in the tent door, which was behind him."* Genesis 18:9-10

Again the Lord said, *"Is anything too hard for the Lord? At the time appointed I will return unto thee, according to the time of life, and Sarah shall have a son."* Genesis 18:14

O, hallelujah! Say, **I believe!**

Why I'm still writing about Abraham is because he believed God, *"and it was counted unto him for righteousness"* Romans 4:3.

You also said, "I believe" because you believe in God, *"even God, who quickeneth the dead, and calleth those things which be not as though they were."* You believe in him basically for everything and everyone that should be your way of life.

"Therefore it is of faith, that it might be by grace; to the end the promise might be sure to all the seed; not to that only which is of the law, but to that also which is of the faith of Abraham; who is the father of us all,(As it is written, I have made thee a father of many nations,) before him whom he believed, even God, who quickeneth the dead, and calleth those things which be not as though they were. Who against hope believed in hope, that he might become the father of many nations; according to that which was spoken, so shall thy seed be. And being not weak in faith, he considered not his own body now dead, when he was about an hundred years old, neither yet the deadness of Sara's womb: He staggered not at the promise of God through unbelief; but was strong in faith, giving glory to God; And being fully persuaded that, what he had promised, he was able also to perform. And therefore it was imputed to him for righteousness. Now it was not written for his sake alone, that it was imputed to him; But for us also, to whom it shall be imputed, if we believe on him that raised up Jesus our Lord from the dead; Who was delivered for our offences, and was raised again for our justification." Romans 4:16-25

What sticks out above first is faith, grace, promise.

You're able to talk of faith when you're under grace. With the two, faith and grace, the promise is sure or certain to all the seed or all they that believe!

Secondly, it is hope - So shall thy seed be.

Hope is pivotal in our way of life, it energies you. For by it (hope) he considered not his own body now dead, when he was about an hundred years old, neither yet the deadness of Sara's womb. You know God is not done with me yet. He staggered not at the promise of God through unbelief; but was strong in faith, giving glory to God; And being fully persuaded that, what he had promised, he was able also to perform. And therefore it was imputed to him for righteousness. Also when Abraham was tempted to offer Isaac, he was fully persuaded that, God was able to raise him from the dead. Hebrews 11:17-19 says, *"By faith Abraham, when he was tried, offered up Isaac: and he that had received the promises offered up his only begotten son, Of whom it was said, That in Isaac shall thy seed be called: Accounting that God was able to raise him up, even from the dead; from whence also he received him in a figure."* And because he hoped; *"therefore it was imputed to him for righteousness. Now it was not written for his sake alone, that it was imputed to him; But for us also, to whom it shall be imputed, if we believe on him that raised up Jesus our Lord from the dead; Who was delivered for our offences, and was raised again for our justification."*

Your faith is not a standalone faith, but is because you *"believe on him that raised up Jesus our Lord from the dead; Who was delivered for our offences, and was raised again for our justification"* Romans 4:24-25. Paul says, *"For this cause I bow my knees unto the Father of our Lord Jesus Christ, Of whom the whole family in heaven and earth is named, That he would grant you, according to the riches of his glory, to be strengthened with might by his Spirit in the inner man; That Christ may dwell in your hearts by faith; that ye, being rooted and grounded in love, May be able to comprehend with all saints what is the breadth, and length, and depth, and height; And to know the love of Christ, which passeth knowledge, that ye might be filled with all the fullness of God"* Ephesians 3:14-19.

When we say believe, it's not like you're left on your own, but you're strengthened with might by his Spirit in the inner man, Christ dwells in your heart by faith, that you may be rooted and grounded in love, and comprehend with all saints what is the breadth, and length, and depth, and height of the fullness of God and of the love of Christ, which passeth knowledge. He said, *"I will not leave you comfortless: I will come to you."* John 14:18.

In John 15:4-5 Jesus says, *"Abide in me, and I in you. As the branch cannot bear fruit of itself, except it abide in the vine; no more can ye, except ye abide in me. I am the vine, ye are the branches: He that abideth in me, and I in him, the same bringeth forth much fruit: for without me ye can do nothing."*

He has put you in his heart; you're being kept and none of you will be lost as long as you abide or stay with his word - he's busy sanctifying us by his word, *"I in them, and thou in me, that they may be made perfect in one; and that the world may know that thou hast sent me, and hast loved them, as thou hast loved me."* John 17:23. It's God that works in us both to will and to do of his good pleasure.

Listen to these scripture verses and memorise them if you can;

"And this is his commandment, That we should believe on the name of his Son Jesus Christ, and love one another, as he gave us commandment." 1 John 3:23

"For God so loved the world, that he gave his only begotten Son, that whosoever believeth in him should not perish, but have everlasting life." John 3:16

"These things have I written unto you that believe on the name of the Son of God; that ye may know that ye have eternal life, and that ye may

believe on the name of the Son of God." 1 John 5:13

"But as many as received him, to them gave he power to become the sons of God, even to them that believe on his name: Which were born, not of blood, nor of the will of the flesh, nor of the will of man, but of God." John 1:12-13

"That if thou shalt confess with thy mouth the Lord Jesus, and shalt believe in thine heart that God hath raised him from the dead, thou shalt be saved. For with the heart man believeth unto righteousness; and with the mouth confession is made unto salvation." Romans 10:9-10

"He that hath the Son hath life; and he that hath not the Son of God hath not life." 1 John 5:12

"For the scripture saith, Whosoever believeth on him shall not be ashamed." Romans 10:11

"Who is he that overcometh the world, but he that believeth that Jesus is the Son of God?" 1 John 5:5

Believe that he is

Your life will be transformed when you believe. Jesus asked his disciples, *"Are ye able to drink of the cup that I shall drink of, and to be baptized with the baptism that I am baptized with? They say unto him, we are able. And he saith unto them, Ye shall drink indeed of my cup, and be baptized with the baptism that I am baptized with..."* Matthew 20:22-23

You'll crossover only if you believe, for *"without faith it is impossible to please him: for he that cometh to God must believe that he is, and that he is a rewarder of them that diligently seek him."*

Jesus said, *"...Verily, verily, I say unto you, Hereafter ye shall see heaven open, and the angels of God ascending and descending upon the Son of man."* John 1:51

It's not everyone that will see, but only they who believe.

Faith doesn't have to be elephant like for it to work. Whatever the size, believing that God is, will give it the motion. Do you believe? Now, you're probably saying, *"Lord, I believe; help thou mine unbelief."* Mark 9:24.

Many believers struggle with unbelief; it is possible to believe, but at the same time not believe, and this is what many of us do, as was the situation with that parent.

Probably, you're reading this because you believe, and that step will take you to another level/dimension of faith. Faith comes by hearing, and hearing the word of God.

Now, you've to master this concept; before you crossover you will need to pass the test, if you don't, you'll remain on this side Jordan until you pass that test. It is as simple as that. In this test you need to demonstrate that you believe.

"…he that cometh to God must believe that he is, and that he is a rewarder of them that diligently seek him." Hebrews 11:6

It's a test that everyone is expected to pass, in order for God to remove all unbearable hindrances and barriers in your way. You don't need to pass with a distinction though. *"Jesus said unto them…for verily I say unto you, If ye have faith as a grain of mustard seed, ye shall say unto this mountain, Remove hence to yonder place; and it shall remove; and nothing shall be impossible unto you"* (Matthew 17:20)

You don't need a gigantic faith to believe, but simply hear – believe – trust.

The bible says, *"And it came to pass after these things, that God did tempt Abraham, and said unto him, Abraham: and he said, Behold, here I am. And he said, Take now thy son, thine only son Isaac, whom thou lovest, and get thee into the land of Moriah; and offer him there for a burnt offering upon one of the mountains which I will tell thee of."* Genesis 22:1-2

His faith was tested, and so will yours. Here is how Abraham passed; he did as he was instructed, and in verse 12 God said, *"Lay not thine hand upon the lad, neither do thou anything unto him: for now I know that thou fearest God, seeing thou hast not withheld thy son, thine only son from me."* While we talk of the faith of Abraham – this is it folks.

Believing God requires your total dependence on him, and obedience and commitment to too; you got to prove your faithfulness to the Lord, that him only will you serve. Show that you can wait for him and be chargeable – Christ carried his cross. Cooperate with him to the point of death. If he says go spy, you go spy. Trust him through it all.

When you come to God believe…

The bible urges us to walk in the steps of faith of our father Abraham, and we saw what Abraham did above. Then it says, *"Therefore it is of faith, that it might be by grace; to the end the promise might be sure to all the seed…"* Romans 4:16

I hear people talk of grace; it's faith that takes you there, and faith is mere believing that God is, and that he's able.

When you come to God, believe that he's. Come to him confidently believing and with complete faith trusting – that he is able.

Abraham, *"….before him whom he believed, even God, who quickeneth the dead, and calleth those things which be not as though they were. Who against hope believed in hope…according to that which was spoken…being not weak in faith…he staggered not at the promise of God through unbelief; but was strong in faith, giving glory to God; And being fully persuaded that, what he had promised, he was able also to perform."* Romans 4:17-21

He that comes to him must believe….

"…it shall be imputed, if we believe on him that raised up Jesus our Lord from the dead."

Hear – believe – call

"For whosoever shall call upon the name of the Lord shall be saved. How then shall they call on him in whom they have not believed? and how shall they believe in him of whom they have not heard? and how shall they hear without a preacher? And how shall they preach, except they be sent? as it is written, How beautiful are the feet of them that preach the gospel of peace, and bring glad tidings of good things! But they have not all obeyed the gospel. For Esaias saith, Lord, who hath believed our report? So then faith cometh by hearing, and hearing by the word of God." Romans 10:13-17

Yes, faith comes by hearing, and hearing by the word of God; hear right, then act upon that you hear. If you hear right, you'll see alright, and that you hear, will bring you to your desired haven.

Rely on his saving knowledge despite the test or trail you go through. God himself even tries you. The word you hear is sometimes delivered to test you.

Prayer of Salvation

Have you ever made Jesus the Lord and Saviour of your life? If not, pray this prayer and start a new life in Christ.

Dear God in heaven,

I come to you in the Name of Jesus. I admit that I am not right with you, and I want to be right with you. I ask you to forgive me of all my sins, and come into my heart and change me. The Bible says if I confess with my mouth that "Jesus is Lord," and believes in my heart that God raised Him from the dead; I will be saved (Rom. 10:9). I believe with my heart and I confess with my mouth that Jesus is the Lord and Saviour of my life. Thank you for saving me and help come off unbelief in Jesus' Name I pray. Amen.

If you prayed this prayer for the first time, I would also like to know. Please send me an email and share your testimony.

WALKING WITH GOD

My desire is to help the saints in their spiritual growth so that they may further get established in the faith. Anyone with Christ has the answer to the world's deepest needs. He/she has the cure to the disease of sin, and the way to escape the eternal horrors of hell, and has the guarantee of everlasting happiness with God.

This puts every believer under a solemn obligation to share the good news with everyone that we come across.

Walking with God!

"He hath shewed thee, O man, what is good; and what doth the Lord require of thee, but to do justly, and to love mercy, and to walk humbly with thy God?" Micah 6:8

Walking with God is not an activity reserved only for the so called men of the cloth. His desire is all his children walk with Him. Moses said, *"would God that all the Lord's people were prophets, and that the Lord would put his spirit upon them!"* Numbers 11:29

Walking with God means He becomes everything to you, and your heart's greatest desire. You get to know Him personally, hear His voice, and share your heart with Him, and you seek to please Him.

When you walk with God means that you and God are in agreement. *"Can two walk together, except they be agreed?"* (Amos 3:3). To walk with God means you have aligned your will with His and seek every day to consider yourself *"crucified with Christ"* (Galatians 2:20). You don't have to be perfect, as none of us are (Romans 3:10). But your heart's desire will be to please to God, and willing to let His Spirit conform you to the image of His Son (Romans 8:29).

Walking with God is often called *"walking in the Spirit"* (Galatians 5:16; Romans 8:4). To walk with God means we choose to glorify Him in every way we can, regardless of personal cost.

It is not difficult to identify people who walk with God. There are several people described as *"walking with God"* in the Bible, beginning with Enoch in Genesis 5:24. Noah is also described as *"a righteous man, blameless among the people of his time, and he walked faithfully with God* (Genesis 6:9). The Lord appeared to Abram, *"and said unto him, I am the Almighty God; walk before me, and be thou perfect."* Genesis 17:1

Behold our calling brethren, it is to walk with God and be *"blameless and harmless, the sons of God, without rebuke, in the midst of a crooked and perverse nation, among whom ye shine as lights in the world,* Philippians 2:15.

Paul says, *"they that are Christ's have crucified the flesh with the affections and lusts, Galatians 5:24. They produce "the fruit of the Spirit [which] is love, joy, peace, longsuffering, gentleness, goodness, faith, meekness, temperance,* Galatians 5:22 -23. When we walk with God every day, the world cannot help but recognise God at work through you.

Think soberly

The body of Christ is ginormous; we are all parts of the same. It takes every one of us to complete it. We belong to each other, and each needs all the others. For you to play your part, think soberly, and know where you fit in.

We all have work to do, and for you to do your work effectively, you should be honest in how you estimate yourself, *"measuring your value by how much faith God has given you."* Know exactly how much you're worth so you can serve accordingly. Do not over or under estimate yourself.

"...think soberly, according as God hath dealt to every man the measure of faith." Romans 12:3

Here we are talking of faith you already have, not that you believe God for. If you don't know, learn now how to, calculate how much you're worth, seek wisdom, guidance, and strength so that you can know how, when, where you stand.

As far as service is concerned it's your own experiences with the Lord that is important. Don't copy the behaviour of others, be yourself. Don't try to get into the good graces of others.

Prove what is good, acceptable and the perfect will of God for yourself and others too. Don't only think of strengthening your-self while in church, but think soberly, pray less in tongues but pray in tune along with the others... *"We, being many, are one body in Christ, and everyone members one of another."* Romans 12:5. You don't exist in a vacuum. Each time you pray in tongues in church know that you're not serving, but probably are selfish.

Having then gifts differing according to the grace that is given to us, serve.

Gifts are abilities you do certain things well with.

Whether it's prophecy, let us prophesy according to the proportion of faith.

"...he that prophesieth edifieth the church" (1 Corinthians 14:4). He helps others to grow in the Lord, encouraging and comforting them. Paul says, *"Follow after charity, and desire spiritual gifts, but rather that ye may prophesy."* 1 Corinthians 14:1

Whenever you can; receive from God and prophesy well. If it's;

- Ministry - serve well
- Teaching - teach well, do a good job of teaching
- Exhorting, preach well, see to it that your sermons are strong and helpful
- Giving - give well, be generous,
- Leading - administer well, take responsibility seriously
- Caring - comfort well, with cheerfulness, share others' grief,
- Love - love we'll, with sincerity, brotherly affectionate, active (stand on the side of good).
- Devotion - pray well, in spirit and truth, hope constantly, and have confidence in Christ.
- Work - work well, happily, hospitably

"Be of the same mind one toward another. Mind not high things, but condescend to men of low estate. Be not wise in your own conceits." Romans 12:16

And last but not least, associate with humble people!

Who are you?

Straight answer from Jesus;

"Ye are the salt of the earth....Ye are the light of the world..." Matthew 5:13-14

Salt because you're precious and valued; you influence, season and preserve lives, and Light, because you can't be hid; you give light to all. You're a light giver.

The world needs you; it cannot get light except it receives it through us! The purpose of light is to illuminate and expose the evil in the world. But light itself must first be exposed before it is to be of any use to the world – if it is hidden, it is no longer useful. When exposed; with it we season world. This light and salt is nothing else but our pure hearts, poor spirit, meekness, mercifulness, our thirsty for righteousness, and peacefulness.

The symbol of salt and light reminds us that the life marked by the blessings associated with the above characteristics is not to be lived in isolation. Jesus wants them to be our manifesto before the world. To be sons, children of God, and to see God you got to earn it.

"Ye are the light of the world. A city that is set on an hill cannot be hid." Matthew 5:14

In the same way, Jesus wants his own people to live visible lives that attract attention to the beauty of God's work in their lives.

He said, "*Blessed are they that mourn: for they shall be comforted.*" Matthew 5:4.

What do you think the world will do to the poor in spirit, the meek, the merciful, and the pure in heart, the peacemakers? To the hungry and they that mourn? They'll persecute them of course!

But "*Blessed are they which are persecuted for righteousness' sake: for theirs is the kingdom of heaven. Blessed are ye, when men shall revile you, and persecute you, and shall say all manner of evil against you falsely, for my sake. Rejoice, and be exceeding glad: for great is your reward in heaven: for so persecuted they the prophets which were before you.*" Matthew 5:10-12

The bible says, "*And seeing the multitudes, he went up into a mountain: and when he was set...he opened his mouth, and taught them...*" Matthew 5:1-2

Blessed are ye, when men shall revile you, and persecute you, and shall say all manner of evil against you falsely, for his sake.

What do you think the world will do to the poor in spirit, the meek, the merciful, and the pure in heart, the peacemakers? The hungry, or they that mourn? When you think the world should gladly receive these, instead they persecute them (Of whom the world was not worthy:) Hebrews 11:38.

But Rejoice! And be exceeding glad: for great is your reward in heaven for;

- you shall be comforted,
- you shall inherit the earth,
- you shall obtain mercy,

- you shall be filled,
- you shall see God,
- you shall be called the children of God
- you shall inherit the earth

Paul says, *"But unto every one of us is given grace according to the measure of the gift of Christ. Wherefore he saith, When he ascended up on high, he led captivity captive, and gave gifts unto men."* Ephesians 4:8

"Then Peter began to say unto him, Lo, we have left all, and have followed thee. And Jesus answered and said, Verily I say unto you, There is no man that hath left house, or brethren, or sisters, or father, or mother, or wife, or children, or lands, for my sake, and the gospel's, But he shall receive an hundredfold now in this time, houses, and brethren, and sisters, and mothers, and children, and lands, with persecutions; and in the world to come eternal life." Mark 10:28-30

*Anoint thine eyes with eyesalve,
that thou mayest see.*

"And unto the angel of the church of the Laodiceans write; These things saith the Amen, the faithful and true witness, the beginning of the creation of God....Because thou sayest, I am rich, and increased with goods, and have need of nothing; and knowest not that thou art wretched, and miserable, and poor, and blind, and naked: I counsel thee to buy of me gold tried in the fire, that thou mayest be rich; and white raiment, that thou mayest be clothed, and that the shame of thy nakedness do not appear; and anoint thine eyes with eyesalve, that thou mayest see." Revelation 3:14, 17-18

Paul said to the Galatians; I fear for you! He said, "*They zealously affect you, but not well; yea, they would exclude you, that ye might affect them. But it is good to be zealously affected always in a good thing, and not only when I am present with you.*" Galatians 4:17-18

He asked, "*Where is then the blessedness ye spake of?*" Galatians 4:15

If you are blind, you can't look at yourself and see that you are wretched, miserable, poor, and naked. Mental darkness is worse than a loss of sight; but a loss of spiritual vision is even worse.

Jesus says, "*...thou sayest, I am rich, and increased with goods, and have need of nothing; and knowest not that thou art wretched, and miserable, and poor, and blind, and naked...*"

It's sad some Christians are the opposite of what they profess. Instead of a blessed life they are wretched, miserable, poor, blind, and naked.

When they say we are rich, we've have wealth and have need of nothing, what they say about themselves is far from truth.

The church at Laodicea looked at their spiritual condition and said we have need of nothing! We're rich, wealthy and blessed! These did not know that they were wretched, miserable, poor, blind, and naked. The contrast between what they thought that they were and what they really were, what they saw and what Jesus sees was surprisingly huge.

What Jesus sees in you is more important than how you see yourself. You may think you're very poor but before him you're really rich.

Be not be deceived by material prosperity, in outward luxury, and in physical health. It may appear like you don't need anything but to be honest you're in dire need.

He said, "I counsel thee to buy of me gold tried in the fire, that thou mayest be rich; and white raiment, that thou mayest be clothed, and that the shame of thy nakedness do not appear; and anoint thine eyes with eyesalve, that thou mayest see."

Tempted by the devil

"Then was Jesus led up of the Spirit into the wilderness to be tempted of the devil." Matthew 4:1

The truth is the Holy Spirit cannot tempt us (James 1:13), but He may lead us to a place where we will be tempted to prove something to us and to the spiritual beings watching us. *"And the Lord said unto Satan, Hast thou considered my servant Job, that there is none like him in the earth, a perfect and an upright man, one that feareth God, and escheweth evil?"* Job 1:8

Temptation is a matter of when for everyone. Jesus' temptation was more brutal and ruthless because He was tempted by the devil himself, not the lesser demons which we sometimes have to face.

"And when the tempter came to him, he said, if thou be the Son of God, command that these stones be made bread. But he answered and said, It is written, Man shall not live by bread alone, but by every word that proceedeth out of the mouth of God." Matthew 4:3-4

Please note; it says, *"...when the tempter came to him..."*. In our lives, it is not a question of if the tempter will come, but when he will come.

It comes simply as this, *"If You are the Son of God..."* if God has sent you Mr. preacher man, then prove it through miracles. Command that these stones become bread.

At that instance many preachers fail God. Why? They bow down to the demands of Satan, for at Satan's suggestions they used God's gifts for selfish purposes, to satisfy own needs. Satan suggested Jesus to use miracle powers to provide food for Him. Jesus would not command that stones become bread, especially at the demand of Satan. We could say that the same temptation came to Jesus on the cross (Matthew 27:40).

Jesus didn't silently disagree with Satan; He answered him from the Word of God. Jesus shows that every word that proceeds from the mouth of God should be more precious to us than food itself.

What Satan proposed made sense, but that written makes even more sense, submitting to His Father's will in all things.

We all can fight our battles in the same way he did. He laid us an example! By relying on the power and truth of God's Word, we can overpower the enemy. Jesus used Scripture to battle Satan's temptation, not some elaborate spiritual power inaccessible to us. Jesus fought this battle saying 'it is written', and He used the word of God as a weapon against Satan and temptation. He used a weapon that one can use when they are all alone.

We effectively resist temptation in the same way Jesus did: by countering Satan's seductive lies by shining the light of God's truth upon them. If we are ignorant of God's truth, we are poorly armed in the fight against temptation.

The second temptation: an appeal to the pride of life.

"Then the devil taketh him up into the holy city, and setteth him on a pinnacle of the temple, And saith unto him, If thou be the Son of God,

cast thyself down: for it is written, He shall give his angels charge concerning thee: and in their hands they shall bear thee up, lest at any time thou dash thy foot against a stone. Jesus said unto him, It is written again, Thou shalt not tempt the Lord thy God." Matthew 4:5-7

If thou be the Son of God, cast thyself down: for it is written.

So many believers have cast themselves down and some so low on the order of the devil.

For it is written: the devil can use this clause also, 'it is written'. The devil has also memorised the Bible, so that he can quote it out of context to confuse, and defeat those he tempts. Jesus knew that Satan was twisting scripture.

But, sadly, nowadays many believers are willing to believe anyone who quotes anything from the Bible. Some have just turned themselves as messengers of the devil. They defend sin with a passion. I told one of my friends to not reduce himself so. I said you're not a preacher of sin but righteousness. A preacher can pretty much say whatever he wants if he first quotes a scripture, and people will assume that he really speaks from the Bible. It is important for each Christian to know the Bible for themselves, and not to be deceived by someone who quotes the Bible but not accurately represent it with correct application.

"Jesus said unto him, It is written again, Thou shalt not tempt the Lord thy God." Matthew 4:7

He replied with Scripture, but applied it correctly. He knew that attempting to manipulate God into such a demonstration would tempt God, which the Scriptures strictly forbid.

This warns us against demanding something spectacular from God to prove His love for us. He has already given the ultimate demonstration at the cross (Romans 5:8), and He can do nothing more spectacular for this generation than that already done.

Your focus should be on your relationship with God, that as a son you've complete confidence in him.

The third temptation: an appeal to the lust of the eyes.

"Again, the devil taketh him up into an exceeding high mountain, and sheweth him all the kingdoms of the world, and the glory of them; And saith unto him, All these things will I give thee, if thou wilt fall down and worship me. Then saith Jesus unto him, Get thee hence, Satan: for it is written, Thou shalt worship the Lord thy God, and him only shalt thou serve." Matthew 4:8-10

1 Corinthians 3:13 says, *"Every man's work shall be made manifest: for the day shall declare it, because it shall be revealed by fire; and the fire shall try every man's work of what sort it is." "For nothing is secret, that shall not be made manifest; neither any thing hid, that shall not be known and come abroad."* Luke 8:17

Satan still thinks his agenda is still secret, but here it has been revealed; it's worship he wants and recognition, far above the kingdoms of the world and their glory. He wants you to bow down on him.

His intentions are manifest; he still wants to ascend into heaven, so he can exalt his throne above the stars of God. He wants to be like the Most High. (Isaiah 14:13-14)

He knows all things belong to God; one day they'll be taken from him anyway, *"the saints of the most High shall take the kingdom, and possess the kingdom forever, even forever and ever."* Daniel 7:18. God allows Satan to function as the god of this age (2 Corinthians 4:4) for a purpose.

For it is written: Jesus replied with Scripture again, and commanded the devil to leave. In the same way we can resist the devil and he will flee from you (James 4:7). It worked for Jesus (Then the devil left Him) and it will work for us.

No son of God can worship the devil so away with you, Satan!

The temptations of Jesus remind us that it is no sin to be tempted, as long as the temptation is resisted.

UNDERSTANDING PRAYER

When faced with a situation, I first ask myself, what does the Bible say about my situation?

Romans 8:26-27 says, *"Likewise the Spirit also helpeth our infirmities: for we know not what we should pray for as we ought: but the Spirit itself maketh intercession for us with groanings which cannot be uttered. And he that searcheth the hearts knoweth what is the mind of the Spirit, because he maketh intercession for the saints according to the will of God."*

I want to pray, but what does the Bible teach concerning prayer?

"...ye have not, because ye ask not. Ye ask, and receive not, because ye ask amiss, that ye may consume it upon your lusts." James 4:2-3

There are two laws of prayer;

1. You do not have because you do not ask, James 4:2.

2. You ask and do not receive because you ask wrongly, James 4:3.

The first one depends on God's love and power: God will give you everything you ask for in Jesus' name. Did Christ really teach this?

Think about these verses:

- Everyone who asks receives, Matthew 7:7, 8.
- If you ask anything in my name, I will do it, John 14:14.
- If you ask anything of the Father in my name, He will give it you, John 16:23.

These wonderful verses and many more of them show us the first law of prayer.

But the second law limits the first. It is based on the wisdom and holiness of God. His love and power must work with His wisdom and holiness.

The second law says that: God will only give His children what is best for them.

Your Father will give good things to them that ask Him, not a stone or a serpent, Matthew 7:9-11.
That the Father may be glorified in the Son, John 14:13.
If my prayer does not glorify the Father, I should not ask. If I do ask, the Son will not give me what I asked for.

That your joy may be full, John 16:24.

I may pray for something I think will bring me pleasure. But instead of giving me what I asked for, God will give me something else that will bring me full joy now and for eternity as well.

The great problem about prayer is: If I pray for something I want, will God give it? The answer is: Yes, unless it is not according to

His will.

These two laws show why this is so.

God answered prayer for many people in Bible times. He still does. Sometimes he refused. He still does.

For example:

Moses prayed that he might lead the people of Israel into the promised land, but God refused, Deuteronomy 3:23-26.

David prayed that his child might live, but God refused, 2 Samuel 12:16,19.

Paul prayed that his thorn in the flesh might be taken away, but God refused, 2 Corinthians 12:8,9.

Sometimes God answered a prayer later on and so received more glory than He would have if He had answered it right away.

The ruler of the synagogue prayed that his daughter might be healed. She died, but Christ raised her again from the dead, Mark 5:23,35-42.

Mary and Martha told Jesus that their brother was sick. Jesus arrived after Lazarus had died, and raised him to life, John 11:3,14,44.

There is great power in prayer.

Even when the Lord Jesus prayed, He added, "Not my will but thine be done", Luke 22:42.

He sometimes answers prayer that is not prayed according to His will.

For example:

The people of Israel grumbled about the food God had given them and asked for meat to eat. God gave it to them, but punished them too, Psalm 106:15.

The men of Gadara asked Jesus to go away, and He did! Mark 5:17.

Prayer is a wonderful benefit, but we must be careful what we pray for.

Whenever we bow in prayer, Christ asks, as it were,
What do you want me to do for you? Matthew 20:32.
And: Do you believe that I am able to do this? Matthew 9:28.

"But the end of all things is at hand: be ye therefore sober, and watch unto prayer." 1 Peter 4:7

Paul in Philippians 4:6 says. "Be careful for nothing; but in every thing by prayer and supplication with thanksgiving let your requests be made known unto God."

This happens when you pray;

• You'll be investing in your account. No word said is wasted; no moth is able to corrupt it. If you'll be able to ask Joseph he will tell you to dream big when you pray! With each deposit made, in your lean years you will leap for joy. You're sowing seeds for a bumper harvest tomorrow. You're not saying idle words; every single word is logged in His book of remembrance. Praying according to his word is same as saying; Father let your will be done. Now read Joshua 4 and let's pray;

Example Prayer 1

Dear Lord God,

I make a commitment to abide by you instructions that I keep space Lord, between me and your ark. You want me to seek guidance, to wait for your lead, to follow after you because you know the way, but even though it's my life l admit I don't, Lord.

Lord God, I seek to know you more and your will, that it done, O Lord, when your spirit speaks to me, I will trust you and obey, and I'll say yes Lord yes the way through Lord.

I thank you Lord for sanctifying me whole from all worldly influences and uncleanliness. Thank you for washing me by the precious blood of your beloved Son. This you've done so that you may prepare me as a ready vessel for your use, miracles and wonders Lord; and now I know, that reading and hearing your word is the only way I shall know that the living God is among us, and is with me, and is the same way that without doubt you'll dispel all darkness, and without fail will drive out our enemies from before us. Father I thank you for being my shield and buckler.

O Lord God, I treasure your word so much. I now know why you want me to keep your word, and why it shouldn't depart from my mouth, it is because through your word we come to see the light, and is the only way we shall have good success - only by your word you'll drive away all our fears Lord.

To you O Lord I give the glory, in Jesus' name. Amen

UNDERSTANDING PRAYER 2

First and foremost, your aim should be to know that the Lord hears you when you pray.

Solomon said; *"Hearken therefore unto the supplications of thy servant, and of thy people Israel, which they shall make toward this place: hear thou from thy dwelling place, even from heaven; and when thou hearest, forgive."* 2 Chronicles 6:21

It's such a wonderful experience to know that the Lord looks upon your prayers with such kind respect. 2 Chronicles 6:19 says, *"Have respect therefore to the prayer of thy servant, and to his supplication, O Lord my God, to hearken unto the cry and the prayer which thy servant prayeth before thee:"*

What that means is, it's possible to know what the Lord thinks concerning your prayers, even before you ask.

When Solomon had finished praying, *"the Lord said unto him, I have heard thy prayer and thy supplication, that thou hast made before me..."* 1 Kings 9:3. Our problem these days, we make our prayers in

WhatsApp, facebook or to be heard of or seen of men. With such kind of petitions, we know God's judgement of them even before you ask.

But anyway, don't assume God hears you but I know. Remember that *"faith is the substance of things hoped for, the evidence of things not seen."* Hebrews 11:1. It's the assurance, not the probability or assumption. 1 John 2:21 says, *"I have not written unto you because ye know not the truth, but because ye know it, and that no lie is of the truth."* Now if you know, listen to what Apostle here says, *"These things have I written unto you that believe on the name of the Son of God; that ye may know that ye have eternal life, and that ye may believe on the name of the Son of God. And this is the confidence that we have in him, that, if we ask any thing according to his will, he heareth us: And if we know that he hear us, whatsoever we ask, we know that we have the petitions that we desired of him."* 1 John 5:13-15.

Sometimes believers lack that confidence; that confidence in him, that when we pray he hears us if we pray according to his will. It's not the multitude of what you say that matters when you pray but to pray aright. There is only one way you can know that he hears you; i.e., only when you *"believe on the name of the Son of God;"* it is by him alone you *"know that ye have eternal life."*

UNDERSTANDING PRAYER PART 3

P aul says in, *"Brethren, be not children in understanding: howbeit in malice be ye children, but in understanding be men."* 1 Corinthians 14:20

Now concerning prayer every believer who prays should also understand the dynamics of prayer.

Paul says, *"For though I would desire to glory, I shall not be a fool; for I will say the truth: but now I forbear, lest any man should think of me above that which he seeth me to be, or that he heareth of me. And lest I should be exalted above measure through the abundance of the revelations, there was given to me a thorn in the flesh, the messenger of Satan to buffet me, lest I should be exalted above measure. For this thing I besought the Lord thrice, that it might depart from me. And he said unto me, My grace is sufficient for thee: for my strength is made perfect in weakness. Most gladly therefore will I rather glory in my infirmities, that the power of Christ may rest upon me. Therefore I take pleasure in infirmities, in reproaches, in necessities, in persecutions, in distresses for Christ's sake: for when I am weak, then am I strong."* 2 Corinthians 12:6 - 10

As a believer know that His grace is sufficient you. *"My grace is sufficient for thee: for my strength is made perfect in weakness"* is a *statement of fact. It will be foolish of you to petition God of the things you know he will never grant them to you. Paul said, "For though I would desire to glory, I shall not be a fool."*

He knew the things he would ask God for and what not to, and although we might pretend every believer should know too. Paul said there was given to me a thorn in the flesh, the messenger of Satan to buffet me, lest I should be exalted above measure. For this thing I besought the Lord thrice, that it might depart from me. And he said unto me, My grace is sufficient for thee: for my strength is made perfect in weakness. Most gladly therefore will I rather glory in my infirmities, that the power of Christ may rest upon me. (ref. 2 Corinthians 12:7-9).

You see how sometimes it's given to you that you should glory in your own infirmities, and take pleasure in them; in reproaches, in necessities, in persecutions, in distresses? And no matter how much you beg God to set you free, sometimes they won't go away because they aren't your enemies, the Devil is. Remember, Romans 5:3-6 says, *"And not only so , but we glory in tribulations also: knowing that tribulation worketh patience; And patience, experience; and experience, hope: And hope maketh not ashamed; because the love of God is shed abroad in our hearts by the Holy Ghost which is given unto us. For when we were yet without strength, in due time Christ died for the ungodly."*

We have access by faith into this grace wherein we stand. He says I'm with you in all your troubles; that is all you need. Actually some of us we are better christians than when we have everything. His power shows up best in our weaknesses.

So he said, when you pray say, *"And lead us not into temptation, but deliver us from evil: For thine is the kingdom, and the power, and the glory, for ever. Amen."* Matthew 6:13. He said when thou prayest, thou shalt not be as the hypocrites are : for they love to pray standing in the synagogues and in the corners of the streets, that they may be seen of men, and when they pray they make you believe that infirmities you should take pleasure in that is evil; so are your reproaches, necessities, persecutions, and distresses. Evil is what the enemy unleashes but infirmities are your stepping stops.

When you understand the grace of God you join the company of those who understand a man's life consisteth not in the abundance of the things which he possesseth, like Moses, who *"refused to be called the son of Pharaoh's daughter; Choosing rather to suffer affliction with the people of God, than to enjoy the pleasures of sin for a season."* Hebrews 11:24-25, and *"...and others were tortured, not accepting deliverance; that they might obtain a better resurrection."* Hebrews 11:35.

"Ye ask, and receive not, because ye ask amiss, that ye may consume it upon your lusts." James 4:3

Example prayer 2

Dear friend,

How about you join me in prayer today?

Father God in the name of Jesus,
I want to thank you for the word of life, which also is now part of my life.

Through it I now know that I've eternal life; I would like to thank you for all the promises manifested through your word, even the forgiveness of my sins.

I would like to thank you for the fellowship I now have with you through your Son, Jesus Christ I welcomed in my life. I also thank you for your Holy Spirit in me, who completes my joy. My joy is complete because each day your Spirit makes me understands that you're in my life to lighten my paths.

Your Holy Spirit each day is undertaking, helping me through and through. I promise to walk in the light of your word, worshipping you in spirit and in truth. I reject all works of darkness, to the glory of God the Father.

Thank you dear God for enlightening my path, my joy is complete in Jesus' name, Amen

Eample Prayer 3

Dear friend,

Today is day 2 you're joining me in prayer. Here's how I prayed today;

Father God in the name of Jesus, I want to thank you for the plans you have for me, especially that you want me also to crossover like Joshua. Help me Lord to cooperate with your will as Joshua did, and to fully understand it.

I'd stayed here, with this condition for too long, and your word has just come at the right time that I should take courage and move on. I'll do, Lord. I couldn't wait any longer Lord, sorrowful, lamenting for my loss, and having no hope is sickening. Thank you for visiting me in my misery, you caused me to hope again.

I thank you Lord for persuading me to move forward; to be strong and courageous in this journey. What is that I could have done without you, Lord?

It suffices me to know that I'm not alone, that you're coming with me in this journey of life. It has always been my desire that your word should give me light/direction, just as you've today. Thank you Lord today for opening my understanding, and the company and guidance Lord; I feel encouraged and persuaded to fight my wars with you Lord, especially doing it your way.

I'm not afraid anymore because you're with me! Your Spirit is with me Lord; what can men do to me?

To you Lord be glory and honour in Jesus' name, amen.

Dear friend,

Thank you for these past few days you were able to stand with me in prayer. Just as I thought this'll be it, I cannot leave you this side Jordan. So I'll show you something tomorrow. Please read Joshua 3 and again let's pray;

Dear God in heaven,

Truly you've blessed me with all spiritual blessings; this I'm able to name one by one. So much you've put (delivered) into my hands, both spiritually and physically; the heritage of your saints. This I knew not, that even my enemies do faint because of me. I'm not afraid anymore.

I thank you Lord God for wisdom and revelation knowledge. One thing you want me to do Lord, it is that I go spy the land of my desired haven. Faith with no action is dead. Lord I thank you for raising me people like Rahab who are very revealing and who want to work with me. This other thing I have learned of you Lord; it is that you're no respecter of persons: But in every nation he that feareth you, and worketh right-

eousness, is accepted with you. Forgive my trespasses Lord, of not being kind to those who're good to me, maybe because they follow not our ways. That makes you God, and us mere men, Lord forgive me for being so judgemental and naive.

I thank you Lord for hiding me under your pavilion, against those who seek to do us harm. Thank you that enemies who pursue hard after us will not catch up with us, and again thank you for every wise counsel regardless of its source. To you be glory.

In Jesus' name Lord I pray, Amen

PRAYING TO GOD

Praying is getting an audience with God, not social media as some believers do. On that note, Leviticus 19:12 says, *"And ye shall not swear by my name falsely, neither shalt thou profane the name of thy God: I am the Lord."*
If prayers are offered to God, there must then be a definite and conscious approach to Him, and a realisation also, that He is listening.

There must be power in your prayers also, and power does not mean that your mind is taken up with the thought of your need but his will. You should all the time be connected with God, or his presence. Jesus taught us how to pray, suggesting that when you pray you should not rush to making petitions. Instead He said, "After this manner therefore pray ye: *Our Father which art in heaven, Hallowed be thy name. Thy kingdom come. Thy will be done in earth, as it is in heaven. Give us this day our daily bread. And forgive us our debts, as we forgive our debtors. And lead us not into temptation, but deliver us from evil: For thine is the kingdom, and the power, and the glory, for ever. Amen."* (Matthew 6:9-13). Train yourself to be more taken of Him than be hasty in your petitions. Worship him first, reverence, honour and give him the glory due to his name.

I said above, prayers are offered to God, because Jesus did the same; "*Who in the days of his flesh, when he had offered up prayers and supplications with strong crying and tears unto him that was able to save him from death, and was heard in that he feared.*" Hebrews 5:7

You need the same mindset and energy, and thanks be to God "the Spirit helpeth our infirmities." (Rom 8:26). How did Jesus pray? Whether it was in public or in private He offered up prayers and supplications with strong crying and tears unto him that was able to save him from death, and was heard in that he feared.

He was heard because he didn't take prayer lightly but each time he approached the throne of grace he did it with fear and trembling. Ought you not to do the same? For Jesus, "*Though he were a Son, yet learned he obedience by the things which he suffered; And being made perfect, he became the author of eternal salvation unto all them that obey him.*" (Hebrews 5:8-9). He authored for us how we too ought to pray, not that from us profanity should go forth.

Prayer - when thou prayest, thou shalt not be as the hypocrites!

"*And it came to pass, that, as he was praying in a certain place, when he ceased, one of his disciples said unto him, Lord, teach us to pray, as John also taught his disciples.*" Luke 11:1

Every believer should know how to pray; if you don't know how, don't be afraid to ask, "Lord, teach us to pray, as John also taught his disciples."

Verse 2 - 4 is used as an example of how you would pray.

"*And he said unto them, Which of you shall have a friend, and shall go unto him at midnight, and say unto him, Friend, lend me three loaves.*" Luke 11:5

- access to the father is all-time guaranteed,
- when you ask God, treat him as you would a friend, who will answer.
- remember when born again, you're not anymore an outsider but his own elect.

"I say unto you, though he will not rise and give him, because he is his friend, yet because of his importunity he will rise and give him as many as he needeth." Luke 11:8

- by importunity means you got to be persistent. Because he's a friend, there is no need to be careful how you (ask, knock, seek) because he understands your emotions - "...he will rise and give him as many as he needeth."

See he has made it a principle,

"And I say unto you, Ask, and it shall be given you; seek, and ye shall find; knock, and it shall be opened unto you. For every one that asketh receiveth; and he that seeketh findeth; and to him that knocketh it shall be opened." Luke 11:9-10

The father knows how to give good gifts to them that ask him.

"And he said unto them, When ye pray, say, Our Father which art in heaven, Hallowed be thy name. Thy kingdom come. Thy will be done, as in heaven, so in earth." Luke 11:2

John says something tremendous, each time you worship, the four beasts in heaven says "Amen," The twenty four elders also joins in to worship with you, *"...the four beasts said, Amen. And the four and twenty elders fell down and worshipped him that liveth for ever and ever."* Revelation 5:14

- make sure when you pray that it's a prayer 'heavens' says amen to, and that it's a prayer the twenty four elders prays along with, *"saying with a loud voice, Worthy is the Lamb that was slain to receive power, and riches, and wisdom, and strength, and honour, and glory, and blessing."* Revelation 5:12

Remember, James says, *"Ye ask, and receive not, because ye ask amiss, that ye may consume it upon your lusts."* (James 4:3). Not only so but believers tend to not follow the rules of engagement.

"And when thou prayest, thou shalt not be as the hypocrites are: for they love to pray standing in the synagogues and in the corners of the streets, that they may be seen of men. Verily I say unto you, They have their reward. But thou, when thou prayest, enter into thy closet, and when thou hast shut thy door, pray to thy Father which is in secret; and thy Father which seeth in secret shall reward thee openly. But when ye pray, use not vain repetitions, as the heathen do: for they think that they shall be heard for their much speaking. Be not ye therefore like unto them: for your Father knoweth what things ye have need of, before ye ask him." Matthew 6:5-8

See how David prayed in Psalm 18

First things first; yourself ought to have a relationship with God.

David said, *"The Lord rewarded me according to my righteousness; according to the cleanness of my hands hath he recompensed me. For I have kept the ways of the Lord, and have not wickedly departed from my God. For all his judgments were before me, and I did not put away his statutes from me."* Psalm 18:20-22

Here is how he achieved it;

"I will love thee, O Lord, my strength. The Lord is my rock, and my fortress, and my deliverer; my God, my strength, in whom I will trust;

my buckler, and the horn of my salvation, and my high tower. I will call upon the Lord, who is worthy to be praised: so shall I be saved from mine enemies." (vs 1-3).

He knew no other god; the Lord God was his only strength, rock fortress deliverer, buckler, high tower, horn of salvation, trust and salvation. And he made this declaration; *"I will call upon the Lord, who is worthy to be praised: so shall I be saved from mine enemies."*

And Psalm 91:14-15 says,

"Because he hath set his love upon me, therefore will I deliver him: I will set him on high, because he hath known my name? [15] He shall call upon me, and I will answer him: I will be with him in trouble; I will deliver him, and honour him."

And when there was trouble he said;

"The sorrows of death compassed me, and the floods of ungodly men made me afraid. The sorrows of hell compassed me about: the snares of death prevented me. In my distress I called upon the Lord, and cried unto my God: he heard my voice out of his temple, and my cry came before him, even into his ears." (vs 4-6).

Upon hearing his prayer; then the earth shook and trembled because He was wroth.

- *"The Lord also thundered in the heavens, and the Highest gave his voice; hail stones and coals of fire."* (Psalm 18:13)

Then David said, *"He sent from above, he took me, he drew me out of many waters. He delivered me from my strong enemy, and from them which hated me: for they were too strong for me. They prevented me in the day of my calamity: but the Lord was my stay."* Psalm 18:16-18

It is important that you know how to pray; God himself teaches you; David says. *"He teacheth my hands to war, so that a bow of steel is broken by mine arms."* Psalm 18:34

SUPPORT MUZEMBI HELPING HANDS!

At Muzembi.org we don't just preach it, we also practice pure religion.

Muzembi Helping Hands is a private foundation, established as a nonprofit / charitable trust, with a principal purpose of making grants to organisations, institutions, or individuals for religious, cultural, educational or other charitable purposes.

Your donation to Muzembi Helping Hands Foundation helps us provide essential support, funding and resources to many. We select grantees that together, build momentum for change. If you think we need to invest in people's future; if you want to have a real hand in making things better — donate today and support our efforts.

God bless,
Laurence
muzembi.org/foundation/